LINCOLNWOOD PUBLIC LIBRARY

W9-CEC-468

1 8 16 (4/07) ⓪
1 8 19 (9/13) ⑤

Lincolnwood Library
4000 W. Pratt Ave.
Lincolnwood, IL 60712

LIFTOFF

A PHOTOBIOGRAPHY OF JOHN GLENN
BY DON MITCHELL

NATIONAL GEOGRAPHIC
WASHINGTON, D.C.

For Grace, Logan Adlai, and Ella Ruth—who make life wonderful.—D.M.

Published by the National Geographic Society

John M. Fahey, Jr., *President and Chief Executive Officer*

Gilbert M. Grosvenor, *Chairman of the Board*

Nina D. Hoffman, *Executive Vice President, President, Books and Education Publishing Group*

Ericka Markman, *Senior Vice President, President, Children's Books and Education Publishing Group*

Stephen Mico, *Senior Vice President and Publisher, Children's Books and Education Publishing Group*

Staff for This Book

Nancy Laties Feresten, *Vice President, Editor-in-Chief of Children's Books*

Suzanne Patrick Fonda, *Project Editor*

Bea Jackson, *Design Director, Children's Books and Education Publishing Group*

Margaret Sidlosky, *Illustrations Director, Children's Books and Education Publishing Group*

David M. Seager, *Art Director*

Marty Ittner, *Designer*

Janet Dustin, *Illustrations Editor*

Carl Mehler, *Director of Maps*

Matt Chwastyk and Steven D. Gardner, *Map Production*

Jean Cantu, *Illustrations Specialist*

Priyanka Lamichhane, *Editorial Assistant*

Debbie Haer, *Copy Editor*

Margie Towery, *Indexer*

Rebecca Hinds, *Managing Editor*

R. Gary Colbert, *Production Director*

Lewis R. Bassford, *Production Manager*

Vincent P. Ryan, Maryclare Tracy, *Manufacturing Managers*

Copyright © 2006 Don Mitchell

All rights reserved. Reproduction of the whole or any part of the contents without written permission from the National Geographic Society is strictly prohibited.

Library of Congress Cataloging-in-Publication Data

Mitchell, Don, 1957-

Liftoff : a photobiography of John Glenn / written by Don Mitchell; foreword by John Glenn.

   p. cm.

Includes bibliographical references.

ISBN-10: 0-7922-5899-1 (hardcover)

ISBN-10: 0-7922-5900-9 (library binding)

ISBN-13: 978-0-7922-5889-5 (hardcover)

ISBN-13: 978-0-7922-5900-8 (library binding)

1. Glenn, John, 1921—Portraits—Juvenile literature.
2. Astronauts—United States—Biography—Juvenile literature.
3. Astronautics—Pictorial works—Juvenile literature. I. Title: Liftoff. II. Title.

TL789.85.G6M57 2006

629.450092--dc22

    2005030916

Acknowledgments

Special thanks to John Glenn for so generously taking the time from his extraordinarily busy schedule, not only to write the Foreword for this book, but also to clarify the facts of his remarkable life story. Thanks to John Glenn's long-time senior advisor, Mary Jane Veno, for her invaluable assistance. Thanks also to former Glenn Senate aides Caroline Arnold; Patricia Buckheit (who appears in the photo on pages 50–51 along with Len Weiss and Randy Rydell); Ron Grimes, for the extremely generous use of his vast collection of Glenn memorabilia; Christopher Jennings; and Sebastian O'Kelly. Thanks also to Jeffrey Thomas, John Glenn Archivist at The Ohio State University.

FRONT COVER: John Glenn in his Mercury mission spacesuit prior to his 1962 orbital flight

HALF-TITLE PAGE: Liftoff of John Glenn's *Friendship 7* capsule from Cape Canaveral, Florida, on February 20, 1962

TITLE PAGE: John Glenn relaxing on the deck of the destroyer U.S.S. *Noa* an hour after *Friendship 7*'s splashdown in the Atlantic Ocean

OPPOSITE PAGE: President John F. Kennedy (left), John Glenn, and Major General Leighton Davis in a Florida parade, celebrating the success of *Friendship 7*

BACK COVER: John Glenn in the pressure suit he wore on his 1998 space shuttle *Discovery* flight

Quote sources

Quotes used in this book are from *John Glenn: A Memoir*, by John Glenn with Nick Taylor, except as noted below. For full bibliographic information, see page 63. p. 5: "One of the most exhilarating...themselves." Testimony before the Senate Judiciary Committee on "An Amendment to the Constitution of the United States Authorizing Congress to Prohibit the Physical Desecration of the Flag of the United States" April 28, 1999 (Serial No. J-106-15), Washington, DC: U.S. Government Printing Office, p. 102; p. 23: "junk...for parts." *Moon Shot*, by Alan Shepard and Deke Slayton, p. 80; p. 31: "I believe...to accomplish." Shepard and Slayton, p. 133; p. 34: "Godspeed, John Glenn." *For Spacious Skies*, by Scott Carpenter and Kris Stoever, p. 226; "Oh, that view...tremendous." *FRIENDSHIP 7*, by Robert Godwin, ed., p. 143; p. 36: "The sunset...up above." Godwin, p. 150; p. 46: "probably one...ever met." *Glenn—The Astronaut Who Would Be President*, by Frank Van Riper, p. 218; "one of the hardest...in my life." Van Riper, p. 223; p. 53: "at 36, ...pieces of machinery..." Harrison E. Salisbury, "Jet Flier Crosses U.S. in Record 3 Hours and 23 Minutes," *The New York Times*, July 17, 1957, p. A5; p. 54: "Liftoff of *Discovery*...American legend." *Back in Orbit*, by Scott Montgomery and Timothy R. Gaffney, p. 11; "Godspeed, John Glenn." Jonathan Alter, "Eject Button On Cynicism," *Newsweek*, November 9, 1998, p. 28; p. 58: "I've looked...public service." *Presidential Odyssey of John Glenn*, by Richard F. Fenno, Jr., p. 6; p. 60: "If you ever...the opportunity." Christopher Jennings, interview with the author, February 21, 2005; "Those who have made...that flag." Testimony before the Senate Judiciary Committee on "Letting the People Decide: The Constitutional Amendment Authorizing Congress to Prohibit the Physical Desecration of the Flag of the United States" March 10, 2004 (Serial No. J-108-60) Washington, DC: U.S. Government Printing Office, p. 149; back cover: "People are afraid...idea to me." *Life*, March 3, 1961, p. 26.

The body text of the book is set in Filosofia.
The display text is set in Flexure, Robust ICG and Surf.

For information about special discounts for bulk purchases, please contact National Geographic Books Special Sales at ngspecsales@ngs.org.

Printed in China

One of the most exhilarating things that can ever happen to a man or woman is to be able to represent their country and be called to something, to a purpose larger than themselves.

Senator John Glenn takes a brisk walk along the National Mall in Washington, D.C.
In the background is a photo of Earth he took from space in 1962. Glenn, a pioneer in
space photography, used a small Minolta camera that he purchased at a Florida drugstore.

FOREWORD

It is my hope that reading this book will inspire you to want to help others by becoming actively involved in public service. Convert your curiosity into action by investigating new things and becoming involved with the great issues of our time. Study hard, read widely, travel, and enjoy the arts. Learn about history and current events so you can be an informed citizen.

I was lucky to have a high school civics teacher who had an almost magical way of making history, government, and politics come alive. He made me see how I could exercise my beliefs and change the world for the better—and that I should not let anything stand in the way of accomplishing this goal.

On the day before his tragic death, President Kennedy talked about the need to overcome obstacles in the exploration of space. He related a story told by the Irish writer Frank O'Connor about a wall he and some boyhood friends encountered during a hike. Rather than let it be an obstacle to their journey, they tossed their hats over it and then had no choice but to follow them. Kennedy said, "This Nation has tossed its cap over the wall of space, and we have no choice but to follow it." And follow it we did, to the benefit of all.

For me, the most exhilarating challenge to the human spirit is embodied in the words printed on the maps of the early explorers: terra incognita—unknown territory. That's why I believe President Kennedy's decision to explore space was one of the boldest initiatives ever undertaken by the United States. One of my greatest honors was to serve our country by being the first American to orbit Earth and, years later, by journeying back into space to participate in experiments aimed at benefiting all humankind.

I challenge you to discover something worth "tossing your hat over the wall" for. Then learn everything you can about it, and find ways to actively direct your passion to make the world a better place for everyone.

John Glenn

JOHN HERSCHEL GLENN, JR., was born on July 18, 1921, in his parents' white frame house in Cambridge, Ohio. It was appropriate that this 20th-century flight pioneer was born and raised near the old National Road, which was traveled by America's 19th-century pioneers who ventured from the Atlantic seaboard to the western frontier. Shortly after John's birth, the Glenns moved to the small town of New Concord, east of Columbus, where John's father was a plumber, and his mother, Clara, was a homemaker and rented rooms to students at the local college.

Life in New Concord was American small-town life at its best—a wholesome mixture of patriotism and a strong sense of community, where people looked out for each other yet where individuals relied on their own abilities. The need and desire to defend America and its values were instilled in John early and would stay with him for the rest of his life. His boyhood experiences shaped John's outlook on life and developed in him a desire to want to help others. In New Concord, John Glenn launched a career of exploration and service to his nation that would take him from a small town firmly rooted in America's heartland to the skies and beyond—into outer space.

Among the Glenns' closest friends in New Concord were Dr. Homer Castor, the town dentist, and his wife, Margaret. The Castor's daughter was about a year older than John. Her name was Anna Margaret, but everyone knew her as Annie. As toddlers, Annie and John shared a playpen during family get-togethers. Little did anyone know that over the years the two would become a permanent part of each other's lives. John was taken with this warm and pretty girl with a bright, shy smile. She developed a severe stutter that made speaking difficult, but John never had a problem communicating with Annie. He enjoyed spending time with her. Whenever there was a school function, John and Annie usually paired off as a couple.

Family photos show John Herschel Glenn, Jr., at 4 months (above) and with his sister, Jean, circa 1929 (right). In the background is the Glenn family home in New Concord, Ohio. The house sat high on an embankment overlooking U.S. Route 40, the historic National Road that linked Baltimore, Maryland, and St. Louis, Missouri.

John's mother, Clara Sproat Glenn (top), was a school teacher before she married. John's father (bottom) was in the Army during World War I. When he returned from the battlefields of France, "he saw the need to know and understand the world beyond the cornfields."

Like many other schoolboys, John enjoyed bicycling, swimming, ice-skating, and playing team sports like football, basketball, and baseball. He also enjoyed exploring the natural wonders of rural Ohio and hunting rabbits in the woods outside of town. New Concord didn't have a Boy Scout troop, so John and his friends formed a group they called the Ohio Rangers. The Rangers went camping and taught themselves the skills they needed to enjoy the outdoors.

John was fascinated by the relatively new field of aviation. When he was six years old, John, and virtually every other American, had been captivated by Charles Lindbergh's famous 1927 flight from New York to Paris—the first transatlantic solo flight. Lindbergh symbolized everything Americans expected from their heroes. He had fearlessly and single-handedly con-fronted, and ultimately triumphed over, the unknown. When Lindbergh returned home from Europe, his every move was reported in newspapers and magazines around the country. John couldn't learn enough about the great aviator. One story said that Lindbergh would fly over New Concord on his way to Columbus. John liked to believe that the silver plane he saw flying toward

Ohio's capital city was Lindbergh's.

One summer day when John was eight, he and his father were returning home from a plumbing job when they spotted an old, open cockpit WACO biplane—an early airplane with two wings, one above the other—at a grass-field airport outside of town. John's dad stopped the car so they could take a look.

John Sr. was as much an aviation enthusiast as his son. He had served in France during the First World War and had observed biplanes in aerial combat ("dogfights") over the battle lines. Those planes were similar to the one that was parked in the field.

The pilot was selling rides, an opportunity the two Glenns couldn't resist. John's father paid the pilot some money, and father and son climbed into the plane, sharing a seat in the rear cockpit. They watched as the pilot started the engine by hand-cranking a starter near the nose of the

In 1927, Charles Lindbergh became the first person to fly solo across the Atlantic Ocean from New York to Paris. The flight in the *Spirit of St. Louis* took 33 hours and 30 minutes. His achievement was an important milestone in the history of aviation and captured the imagination of millions, including young John Glenn.

plane before climbing into the front cockpit. John found himself bouncing along the grass airstrip then suddenly launched into the sky. All he could hear was the roar of the engines and the wind rushing by. John was fascinated by the spectacular view of the shrinking landscape and the curious feeling of being suspended in air without falling.

After that flight, John was hooked on flying. When he was riding in the car with his dad, John would stick his cupped hand out the open window and let the wind bend it in different directions, as it does the wing of an airplane.

John (seated second from left in the front row) and the New Concord High School basketball team. He enjoyed playing many sports in school, especially basketball. John "learned to love the game's speed, its constant motion, and its subtle and intricate weave of strategies and plays."

Love of country was a given. Defense of its ideals was an obligation. The opportunity to join in its quests and explorations was a challenge not only to fulfill a sacred duty, but to join a joyous adventure. That feeling sums up my childhood. It forms my beliefs and my sense of responsibility.

Civics teacher Harford Steele (above) was a major inspiration for John to pursue a life of public service. John recalls that when Mr. Steele gripped your shoulder to emphasize a point of discipline, "you knew you'd been gripped."

John also built model airplanes patterned after airplanes flown by traveling stunt pilots called barnstormers. He hung his models from the ceiling of his bedroom and imagined what it would be like to fly real airplanes.

In the 1930s, the Great Depression, which caused massive unemployment and poverty, hit New Concord as hard as it did the rest of the nation. John's father was among the more successful businessmen in town, but the family still struggled. One evening, John was alarmed to overhear his parents whispering that the bank was going to foreclose on their mortgage, and they might lose their home. Like most families, the Glenns had taken out a bank loan called a mortgage to pay for their house. This meant the bank had the right to take possession of the house, or foreclose, if the loan could not be repaid. And the Glenns, like many American families at this time, were having trouble making their monthly mortgage payments.

When John was eight years old, he took his first airplane ride in an old WACO biplane similar to the one shown here.

John was aware that some families in New Concord were having such a difficult time making ends meet that parents had no choice but to send their children away to live with relatives. This was happening all over the country. Luckily his family was able to stay together. They ate fruit and vegetables grown in their garden. (It was John's responsibility to weed and hoe the large family garden, and he hated every minute of it.) Sometimes his father was paid with food rather than money for the plumbing jobs he did. So the family had food to eat but not always enough money to pay all the bills.

Fortunately, the Glenns and countless others who were at risk of losing their homes were helped by President Franklin Roosevelt's New Deal programs. The new Federal Housing Administration backed mortgages with federal insurance that allowed banks to spread payments out over more years. The Glenns qualified for this program and were able to keep their house. These government programs provided John with a firsthand lesson on how government can play a meaningful role in changing people's lives for the better and in helping those who are unable to help themselves. John would apply these lessons one day as a member of the United States Senate.

During this time, John was absorbed with his classes and school activities. One of the greatest influences on John were his teachers in New Concord, especially Harford Steele, his no-nonsense high school civics teacher. Steele had a distinctive way of making history, government, and politics exciting and meaningful. He instilled in John the sense that citizenship was not a right to be taken for granted, but a responsibility that required the active participation of all Americans.

John (age 16) and Annie (age 17) in "the Cruiser," his 1929 Chevrolet convertible. "I don't remember the first time I told Annie that I loved her, or the first time she told me. It was just something we both knew."

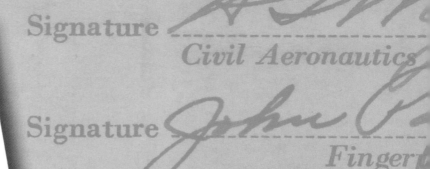

John, in his dress Marine uniform, and Annie shortly after their wedding in New Concord in 1943. In the background is John's first pilot's license, which he earned in 1941 just before his 20th birthday.

[The Marine Corps 'virtues] included hard work, religious faith, and personal discipline. They embraced love of country, love and respect for one's family, a willingness to accept responsibility for one's actions, and a combination of feelings in which brotherhood, courage, and loyalty were all bound up together.

Like most American teenagers, John became preoccupied with auto-mobiles. His father sold automobiles from his plumbing store, and John quickly learned how to drive and repair them. When he turned 16, his dad gave him a battered old 1929 Chevrolet convertible, which he painted maroon. John and Annie nicknamed it "the Cruiser." To John, the old car was almost like having his own set of wings.

As war clouds started to form over Europe in 1939, John enrolled in Muskingum College in New Concord. By attending the local college, he could not only save money on room and board by living at home, but also be with Annie, who was already a student at the college.

John volunteered for a government-sponsored civilian pilot training program to prepare for a war that seemed increasingly likely to involve the United States. Students who successfully completed the program would receive their pilot's license and college credit. The flight training was rigorous. As John mastered increasingly complicated maneuvers, he discovered that flying came naturally to him. And more importantly, he loved it. By July 1941, just before his 20th birthday, John Glenn earned his pilot's license.

The outside world jolted John and every other American out of the peaceful pattern of their lives on Sunday, December 7, 1941, when Japanese forces attacked the U.S. Pacific fleet at Pearl Harbor, Hawaii. The attack brought the U.S. into World War II. John wasted no time telling Annie and his parents that he intended to enlist in the military. Before leaving New Concord to report for Navy flight training in early 1942, John and Annie became engaged.

John was proud to be a naval aviator. Being able to take off from and land on aircraft carriers required enormous training and skill. But the Marines were at the forefront of the fighting against the Japanese in the Pacific, and that's where John wanted to be.

He was impressed by this elite military organization's pride and esprit de corps—the spirit of devotion and enthusiasm—that was instilled in every Marine during training, not only for each other but also for the Marine Corps as a whole. John learned that a Marine was more afraid of letting his comrades down than of getting hurt himself. This sense of trust and confidence did a lot to explain the Marines' impressive record of military victories. So it was no surprise that when John performed in the top 10 percent of his training class in both ground and air instruction, he applied and was accepted into the Marines. He was commissioned as a second lieutenant.

John returned home on a 15-day leave to marry Annie in New Concord in the spring of 1943. Like many weddings during the war, there were few frills, but it was well-attended by people from the town.

While John was in flight training, Annie turned down a scholarship for a graduate program in music at the prestigious Juilliard School in New York. She wanted to contribute to the war effort, so she went to work as a secretary for the Army in Dayton, Ohio. After their wedding, Annie lived the demanding life of a military spouse, following John around the country to various duty posts and waiting anxiously for him to return from combat overseas.

Their first post was San Diego, California, where John reported for additional flight training. After several weeks, John's squadron was transferred to the Marine Corps Air Station at El Centro, in California's Imperial Valley. There, he and the other pilots learned to fly the F4U Corsair fighter plane. For several days that October, none other than flying legend Charles Lindbergh came to El Centro to brief the squadrons on improvements to the plane. Lindbergh was quiet and reserved, but like many pilots, he became more open and lively when it came to talking about aviation. (He would later join John's squadron in several combat missions in the Pacific.) After completing his training on the Corsair, John was ready for combat.

In early 1944, his squadron was deployed to the Marshall Islands, in the South Pacific. Saying goodbye to Annie was the most difficult part. Trying to be cheerful, he told his new bride: "I'm just going down to the corner

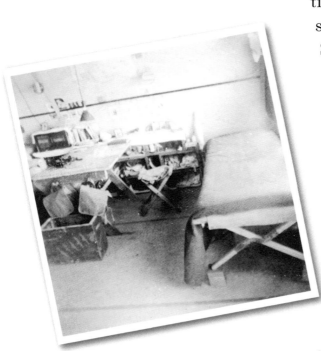

John's modest living quarters on Majuro, in the Marshall Islands, during World War II

store to get a pack of gum."
She bravely replied, "Don't be
long," not knowing when or if
she would ever see him again.

In his first combat mission,
John and his division flew
against a Japanese-held
island, firing machine guns
at enemy anti-aircraft guns
to clear the way for U.S. dive-
bombers. For John it was a
particularly tough initiation
to war. His wingman—and one of his
closest friends—was shot down and
killed. The war had suddenly become
very personal for John.

John, children Lyn and Dave, and Annie
in 1949 after church one Sunday in
Corpus Christi, Texas, where John was a
flight instructor in the Marine Corps

During his tour of duty in the Marshall Islands, John flew 59 missions
and was hit by anti-aircraft fire 5 times. The pilot from New Concord was
rewarded for his courage in combat against the Japanese with 2
Distinguished Flying Crosses and 10 Air Medals.

By the time the war ended in August 1945, John realized that he loved
being a Marine pilot. Rather than return to civilian life, he decided to make
the Marine Corps his career.

John became a flight instructor, and he enjoyed the challenges of his new
job. He and Annie had to get used to the frequent moves to new bases, but at
least they were together. During this time, their lives became fuller as their
family expanded with the birth of their son, David, in 1945, followed by the
birth of their daughter, Lyn, in 1947.

The end of the Second World War ushered in a new era of global tension
called the Cold War that lasted until 1989. It was dominated by two superpowers:
the Union of Soviet Socialist Republics (U.S.S.R.), or Soviet Union, which
wanted to establish communist dictatorships under its control, and the
United States, which was dedicated to stopping the spread of communism.

John (foreground) flying in a formation of F4U Corsairs, the fighter-bomber he flew in World War II and later in China during the winter of 1946–1947

Nothing gave me more pleasure than to be flying the Corsair. At the controls of a small, high performance aircraft day in and day out, you reach a point of oneness with the plane.

Air-to-air combat...was the ultimate in fighter flying, testing yourself against another pilot in the air....You believe you're the best in the air. If you do, you're not cocky, you're combat-ready. If you don't, you'd better find another line of work.

Both sides knew they could destroy each other and much of the world with their arsenals of nuclear weapons. This meant that in addition to maintaining a large supply of nuclear weapons, each side had a large number of troops armed with non-nuclear weapons to respond to fighting wherever it broke out.

This Cold War became a hot war when the communist North Koreans invaded South Korea in June 1950. The United States and the United Nations came to the assistance of South Korea. John felt that his combat flight experience and extensive training shouldn't be wasted on a "desk job." He repeatedly requested to fly in the Korean War, and his request was finally granted. John assured Dave and Lyn that he would return before they knew it. He told Annie, when he said farewell at the airport, "I'm just going to the corner store to get a pack of gum." Annie smiled and again replied, "Don't be long." John shipped out to Korea in February 1953.

Instead of the propeller aircraft he flew in the Second World War, John piloted jet fighters in the Korean War, flying 63 missions with a Marine Fighter Squadron. His plane was hit by enemy gunfire 7 times, though miraculously, he was never injured. Some of these missions were with the already legendary Boston Red Sox baseball player Ted Williams, and they became good friends. These aerial combat missions often took John and his fellow pilots behind enemy lines in barren, mountainous regions of North Korea where they targeted bridges, railroads, and troop and supply staging areas.

John flew 27 combat missions in F-86 Sabrejets as part of an exchange pilot

John, safely back from a combat mission in Korea, stands next to his badly shot-up plane (above). Occasionally, his planes were so damaged that they were judged unflyable and marked by maintenance officers as "junk to be cannibalized for parts."

Boston Red Sox baseball legend Ted Williams (right) flew with John's squadron during the Korean War. According to John, Williams "gave flying the same perfectionist's attention he gave to his hitting."

program with the U.S. Air Force. John shot down three North Korean MiG jet fighters along the Yalu River in the last nine days before a truce ending hostilities came into effect in July 1953. For his aggressive flying tactics, John was dubbed the "MiG Mad Marine" by his fellow pilots. John was awarded two Distinguished Flying Crosses and eight Air Medals for his service in Korea.

When the Korean War was over, John wanted to stay on the cutting edge of aviation by becoming a test pilot. A new generation of fighter jets was being developed. Before these aircraft could enter the military's inventory, they had to be exhaustively tested to prove their safety and combat worthiness. This was dangerous work, but John relished the challenge. After attending Test Pilot School in 1954 at the Naval Air Test Center at Patuxent River, Maryland, he served as a test pilot and project officer on a number of aircraft.

After several years of testing at "Pax River," John was transferred to the Fighter Design Branch of the Navy Bureau of Aeronautics in Washington, D.C., where he served from November 1956 to April 1959. During his time there, John worked on the development of the F-8U Crusader, the new fighter for the U.S. Navy that was to be the first supersonic fighter plane to be based on an aircraft carrier. He became convinced that the best way to demonstrate the Crusader's capabilities was to fly across the country at supersonic speed (faster than the speed of sound)—something that hadn't been done before. Since the Crusader could fly faster than a bullet shot from a .45-caliber pistol (586 miles per hour), John named his proposal Project Bullet. His first hurdle was to persuade his superiors at the Pentagon, the headquarters for the U.S. military near the nation's capital.

John Glenn was a fierce competitor. Like most highly goal-oriented people, he didn't wait for things to happen to him. He *made* things happen. For months, John worked hard to overcome opposition to his proposal, patiently but persistently meeting with officials at the various levels of command to put to rest any doubts or concerns about the proposed mission. Finally, his efforts paid off.

On July 16, 1957, John took off in his F-8U from Los Alamitos Naval Air Station in California. The Crusader had to be refueled in flight three times as it crossed the United States. Two sonic booms (concentrated blasts of

The sonic booms, created by perfect atmospheric conditions over the eastern third of the United States, hit the ground behind me as I flew.... I was just worried about maintaining supersonic speed and getting to New York with enough fuel to land.

MAJOR J.H. GLENN USMC
PROJECT BULLET

John's 1957 transcontinental flight, Project Bullet, sent out sonic booms that rattled communities below his flight path. The sonic booms that thundered over New Concord prompted a neighbor of the Glenn family to run down the street, calling, "Mrs. Glenn, Johnny dropped a bomb! Johnny dropped a bomb!"

For the success of Project Bullet, Major John Glenn received his fifth
Distinguished Flying Cross from Secretary of the Navy Thomas S. Gates.

sound waves created when airplanes travel faster
than the speed of sound) shook New Concord
as he passed overhead on his race to the East
Coast. When he landed at Floyd Bennett Field
on Long Island, New York, he had beaten the previous transcontinental
record by 21 minutes, completing the trip in 3 hours, 23 minutes and 8.4
seconds. The successful completion of the flight earned John his fifth
Distinguished Flying Cross.

The Cold War tension between the United States and the Soviet Union
received a jolt later that same year when the Soviets launched the first Earth-
orbiting satellite, an unmanned spacecraft named Sputnik, on October 4, 1957.

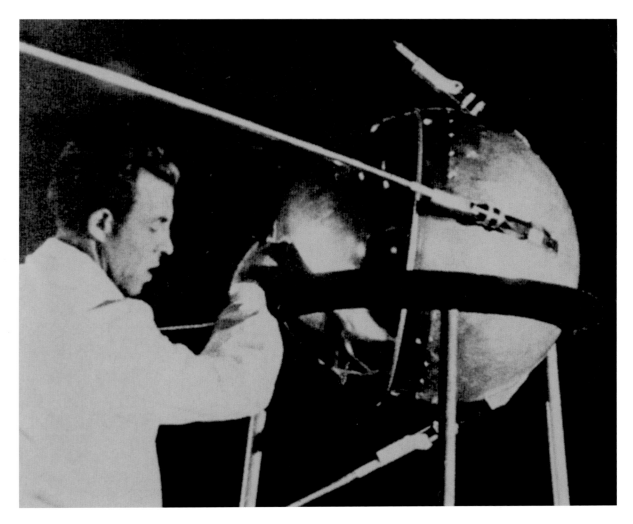

The Soviets' launch of Sputnik in October 1957 marked the beginning of the U.S.–Soviet space race. The world's first satellite weighed only 183 pounds and took about 98 minutes to orbit Earth.

As the satellite circled over the United States, Americans felt threatened by the Soviets' technical achievement. Could the Soviets now spy on the United States from space? Or worse, could they now more easily use rockets to launch nuclear weapons onto U.S. territory? The achievement was a tremendous blow to America's self-image of being the most technologically advanced country in the world. The U.S. Government responded quickly by accelerating its own program to launch a man into space.

In early 1958, the federal government was looking for experienced test pilots to try out for the space program. Becoming part of this program, run by the newly created National Aeronautics and Space Administration (NASA), was the hottest competition for test pilots at this time. John was determined to be selected for the astronaut corps. (The Soviets called their space pilots cosmonauts, while the Americans called their counterparts astronauts.) This first manned space flight project was known as Project Mercury.

No one knew how humans would react to the harsh environment of space, since no humans had ever been in outer space. To insure that the astronauts could perform effectively, the applicants to the space program had to undergo a rigorous battery of physical and psychological testing. The candidates were endlessly poked and prodded by physicians, who made every test and measurement of the human body, both inside and out, that they could devise. The would-be astronauts were shaken, exposed to simulated high altitudes without adequate oxygen or pressure suits, forced to endure extreme heat and cold, and placed in isolation chambers. They were interviewed and assessed

The seven Project Mercury astronauts (left to right): M. Scott Carpenter, L. Gordon "Gordo" Cooper, John Herschel Glenn, Jr., Virgil I. "Gus" Grissom, Walter M. Schirra, Jr., Alan B. Shepard, Jr., and Donald K. "Deke" Slayton.

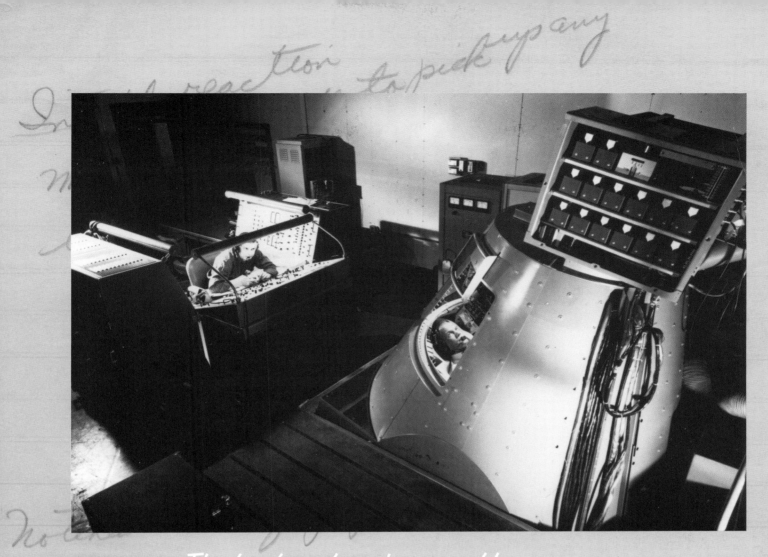

The tests, obnoxious as they were, were fascinating for the most part. It was all in the interests of science, and going into space was going to be one of the greatest scientific adventures of all time.

John takes a turn in the flight procedures trainer at Langley Air Force Base, in Virginia (above), while a technician monitors a simulated space flight. In another test, John was placed in an isolation chamber. To pass the time, he wrote 18 pages of notes (background) in the pitch-black room, making lists and composing poetry.

Soviet Premier Nikita Khrushchev (second from right) and Soviet cosmonauts in Moscow in 1963. Yuri Gagarin stands next to Valentina Tereshkova, who would become the first woman in space. Gherman Titov is second from the left.

by psychiatrists and psychologists to determine their mental processes, including how stable and resistant to panic they were.

As challenging, and sometimes humiliating, as the tests were, John worked hard and endured all of these exams without complaint. On April 6, 1959, he was named as one of the seven-member Mercury team.

Although all of the astronauts were seasoned test pilots, their past experience did not prepare them for the unique dangers of space flight. One of the riskiest parts of astronaut training was preparing for an orbital flight that had to be aborted, or canceled, before it was completed. This could leave an astronaut stranded in the desert or the jungle, far from the planned landing site. The astronaut had to be able to survive for up to 72 hours in extreme conditions until NASA could rescue him. The astronauts were also well aware that many of the booster rockets that NASA was testing to carry them into space had blown up on the launch pad. Knowing about all these dangers, John and the other astronauts were convinced that at least one of them would lose his life in the Mercury program.

John firmly believed that the astronauts were not simply expanding the frontiers of aviation. They were serving as living symbols of the country's future. John felt strongly that they all had an obligation to avoid any behavior—public or private—that would tarnish the program that he considered essential to the nation's future.

The space race reached a new level of competition on April 12, 1961. On that day, Soviet cosmonaut Yuri Gagarin became the first human to travel in space in an orbital flight, which lasted more than one and a half hours. Once again, the Soviets had beaten the Americans.

John, and every other Mercury astronaut, wanted to be the first American in space, but that honor fell to Alan Shepard. Shepard's almost 15-minute flight took place on May 5, 1961, in his *Freedom 7* capsule. It was suborbital, meaning that he did not make a complete orbit of Earth.

The success of Alan Shepard's flight encouraged President Kennedy to challenge the nation to be the first to put a man on the moon. In an address to a joint session of Congress on May 20, he said: "I believe this nation should commit itself to achieving the goal, before this decade is out, of landing a man on the moon and returning him safely to Earth. No single space project in this period will be more impressive to mankind, or more important for the long-range exploration of space, and none will be so difficult or expensive to accomplish." This was a challenge to the Soviets as well, and the superpower space race became even more intense. For the United States, this effort would be called Project Apollo.

Next in space on July 21, 1961, was Mercury astronaut Gus Grissom in his *Liberty Bell 7* spacecraft, which was the second and final suborbital Mercury test flight. This flight lasted just over 15 minutes and almost ended in disaster. After the capsule landed on the water, the hatch blew off prematurely, and the capsule sank into the Atlantic Ocean before it could be recovered. Astronaut Grissom narrowly escaped being drowned.

John was awarded the Marine Corps Astronaut insignia.

The Soviets rose to the challenge. On August 6, 1961, they launched cosmonaut Gherman Titov into space for 17 orbits around Earth. The pressure was now on NASA to go beyond suborbital flights and put an astronaut into Earth orbit. It was John Glenn's turn on the launch pad.

It was important to John that Annie and the children understand the mission and have as much confidence in it as he did. John described everything he could about the space program and his training to his family. One summer, 16-year-old Dave spent several weeks following his father around in the training program. It helped Dave to better understand what his father was going through. John's space capsule needed a name. So he asked Dave and Lyn, who was 14, to come up with one that represented the United States and how the seven Mercury astronauts and other Americans felt about the rest of the world. After a lot of thought, Dave and Lyn's top choice was "Friendship." John thought it was the perfect choice. He named his spacecraft *Friendship 7*.

John never attempted to conceal from his family the dangers of the space program. During the weeks prior to his launch, he took Annie, Dave, and Lyn on a winter picnic at a park in northern Virginia. He raised the possibility that he could die during his flight. John stressed to Dave and Lyn that this mission was important to the country and something he really wanted to do. He didn't want them to be bitter and blame him, NASA, or God if he didn't survive. While John had made an extra effort to communicate with his children about all aspects of his space mission, they were still deeply concerned about their father's safety and somewhat shaken by the possibility that he could be killed.

After tremendous press attention, public anticipation, and 11 delays due to mechanical problems and poor weather conditions, John Glenn prepared to be launched into space on February 20, 1962.

He woke up around 1:30 a.m., shaved, showered, and ate breakfast. A physician examined him and pronounced him fit for launch. Then John was helped into his silver space suit. After so many delays, John wasn't confident that the launch would really happen.

He was shoehorned into the cramped confines of *Friendship 7*, high atop the new Atlas missile. After the capsule was sealed, John was allowed to speak privately

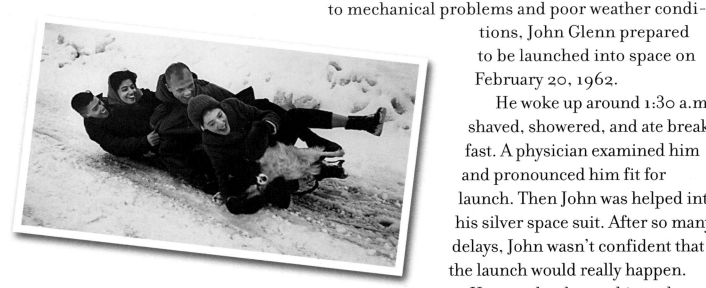

John's military and space careers required frequent absences from his family. When he was home, he made family time a priority. Here, the Glenns, including the family dog Chipper, enjoy the snow in Virginia.

People have always asked if I was afraid.
I wasn't. Constructive
apprehension is more like it.

After many delays, John is wedged into
Friendship 7 early in the morning of February
20, 1962. A postage stamp commemorating
the mission appears in the background.

Thousands of commuters in New York's Grand Central Station pause on their way to work to watch the launch of John Glenn in *Friendship 7*.

through a telephone link to Annie, Dave, and Lyn. "Hey, honey, don't be scared," he said to Annie. "Remember, I'm just going down to the corner store to get a pack of gum." "Don't be long," came her now familiar reply. John promised Annie he would call her later that afternoon after the flight, told her he loved her, and said "goodbye." He was glad no one could see the tears in his eyes.

John wasn't afraid. As he lay in his seat waiting for liftoff, he felt a sense of what he called "constructive apprehension," which meant he was keenly alert to all aspects of his situation, including the risks. John believed that knowledge was the best remedy for fear.

At 9:47 a.m., the Atlas booster rocket carrying John Glenn and *Friendship 7* roared off its Cape Canaveral, Florida, launch pad as millions of Americans watched on television or listened to radio reports. Fellow astronaut and close friend Scott Carpenter gave his parting message, "Godspeed, John Glenn." As the G forces—or gravitational pull—increased, John was smashed into his seat. The booster engines hurled the capsule into orbit, reaching an apogee (farthest point) of more than 160 miles above Earth's surface and a top speed of 17,545 miles per hour.

Within minutes, John experienced weightlessness. "Zero G and I feel fine," he radioed back to Earth. "Capsule is turning around." Through its window, John saw the beautiful blue-green curved horizon of Earth against the vastness of space. Filled with wonder and awe, he exclaimed, "Oh, that view is tremendous!"

Pipes whined and creaked below me; the booster shook and thumped when the crew gimbaled the engines.... We had joked that we were riding into space on a collection of parts supplied by the lowest bidder on a government contract, and I could hear them all.

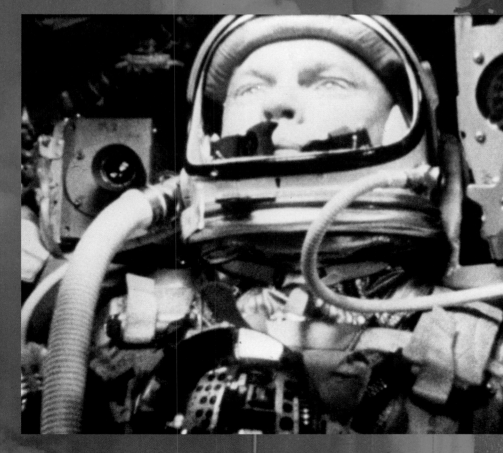

A camera on board *Friendship 7* photographed John during his flight (inset). In the background, the Atlas rocket lifts off from Cape Canaveral's Launch Complex 14.

The sunset was beautiful. It went down very rapidly. I still have a brilliant blue band clear across the horizon almost covering my whole window.... The sky above is absolutely black, completely black. I can see stars though up above.

From his "orbiting front porch,"
John photographed this view of a space
sunset, which he thought "was even
more spectacular than I imagined."

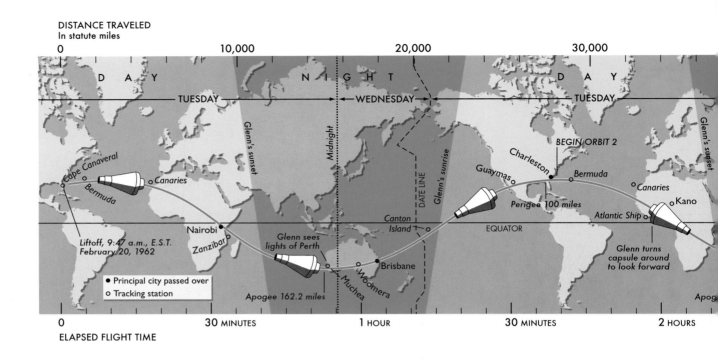

John marveled at the beauty of the multi-colored sunrises and sunsets he observed from space.

But 90 minutes into John's flight, complications developed. Trouble with his automatic control systems forced John to take partial, then full, manual control to keep the capsule stable. Then, during the second orbit of *Friendship 7*, NASA officials believed that the latches holding the spacecraft's heat shield in place might have pulled loose. This wasn't supposed to happen until the last stage of re-entry. At that time, the main parachute would open to slow the craft, and the landing bag would inflate to absorb the shock of hitting the ocean's surface. To guarantee that the heat shield would stay in place, the package of retro-rockets (rockets that are fired to slow the capsule for re-entry) was kept strapped over the shield instead of being released after firing.

The shield's function was to protect the astronaut from the enormous heat produced by the friction created when the spacecraft passed through the atmosphere on its way back to Earth. Without the heat shield, John Glenn would be burned alive during re-entry by temperatures as high as 9,500 degrees Fahrenheit—almost the temperature of the sun's surface.

At first, NASA's Mission Control did not tell John about the specific problem, though they asked him many questions. There was a concern that telling John might cause him to panic. Through the news media, the entire

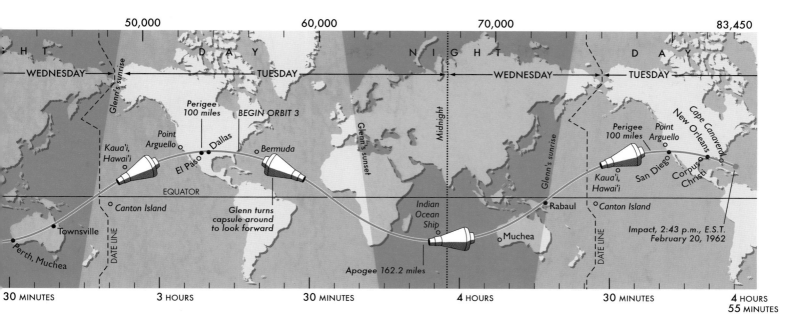

50,000   60,000   70,000   83,450

WEDNESDAY   TUESDAY   WEDNESDAY   TUESDAY

Perigee 100 miles   BEGIN ORBIT 3

Point Arguello
Kaua'i, Hawai'i
El Paso   Dallas
Bermuda

Perigee 100 miles   Point Arguello
Cape Canaveral
New Orleans
Kaua'i, Hawai'i   San Diego   Corpus Christi

EQUATOR

Canton Island

Glenn turns capsule around to look forward

Indian Ocean Ship

Rabaul   Canton Island

Muchea

Townsville

Perth, Muchea

Apogee 162.2 miles

Impact, 2:43 p.m., E.S.T. February 20, 1962

30 MINUTES   3 HOURS   30 MINUTES   4 HOURS   30 MINUTES   4 HOURS 55 MINUTES

John's three Earth orbits and the principal cities and tracking stations he passed over are shown on this map (above). The numbers across the bottom help track where he was during each minute of the flight, from launch to splashdown (impact). The progress of John's flight was closely monitored by Mission Control at Cape Canaveral (top, left) and tracking stations throughout the world. Lyn, Annie, and Dave anxiously watch the television in their Arlington, Virginia, home (bottom, left) as John is launched into space. In the background is Frank Erwin, a minister and family friend.

FEARED   ACTUAL

The diagram at left shows the worst case scenario for *Friendship 7*'s re-entry into Earth's atmosphere. After the retro rockets and their bindings are gone, the loose heat shield slips away, incinerating the capsule in seconds. The right diagram depicts *Friendship 7*'s actual re-entry. The retro pack remains strapped over the heat shield to keep it in place during re-entry.

world had been informed about the heat shield problem before he was. Annie had been notified by NASA that John might not return from the flight because of this problem, adding enormously to her anxiety.

After a short time, NASA officials finally told John about their concerns. Though he didn't say anything at the time, John was angry about having this information concealed from him. He believed that the pilot of any craft should be kept fully informed of all information related to his flight. What if communications with Mission Control had broken down, and he had to make important flight decisions based solely on what he knew on board the spacecraft?

As he completed his third and final orbit, John prepared to fire the retro rockets that would slow down *Friendship 7* for re-entry into the atmosphere. Instead of ejecting the used rockets into space, John was instructed to keep them attached. Strapped to the front of the heat shield, they would hold it in place if there really was a problem. There were some tense moments on the ground when he lost communications with Mission Control as he was coming

Prior to the shuttle program, manned U.S. spacecraft returning to Earth landed in the ocean. Here, the crew of the U.S.S. *Noa* use a steel cable to secure *Friendship 7*. Later it will be used to hoist the craft onto the destroyer's deck. The capsule's periscope is extended just above the ocean's swells. The water has been stained green by a floating dye marker to aid in locating the spacecraft.

through the atmosphere. John witnessed a spectacular fireball through the capsule's window as the retro pack (the used rockets) burned away. To his great relief, the heat shield remained intact, protecting his life.

John's family, NASA officials, and millions of people around the world held their breath, waiting for news of John's safe return to Earth. Finally, the capsule made it through the atmosphere. At precisely 4 hours, 55 minutes, and 23 seconds after launch, splashdown occurred 800 miles southeast of Cape Canaveral. Ships and helicopters raced to the landing site to pluck *Friendship 7* from the sea. After bobbing up and down in the Atlantic Ocean for several minutes, *Friendship 7*, with John Glenn still inside the cramped, hot confines of the capsule, was hoisted aboard the destroyer U.S.S. *Noa* and lowered onto the deck. John requested that the area in front of the capsule be cleared, and then he hit a firing pin and blasted the hatch open. A refreshing

After splashdown, John called Annie from the U.S.S. *Noa* to tell her that he was safe. Just a short time before this call, Annie feared that John had died during the capsule's re-entry into the atmosphere. "Hearing my voice speaking directly to her brought first tears, then audible happiness."

gust of sea air filled his lungs. The moment he stepped onto the ship's deck, John found out what it was like to be the most popular person in the United States.

The tumultuous response to John Glenn's orbital flight was unlike anything seen for an individual since Charles Lindbergh's triumphant return to the United States after his transatlantic solo flight to Paris almost 35 years before. John Glenn's willingness to sacrifice his life for his country time and again—in combat, as a test pilot, and as an astronaut—is a fundamental characteristic of true heroism. And people enthusiastically embraced John for what he was: an authentic American hero.

President Kennedy called to congratulate him. Then John called Annie at their home in Arlington, Virginia, which was besieged by members of the news media. While she knew from watching television that her husband was all right, she sobbed with relief when she heard his voice.

After several days of debriefings and medical tests at Grand Turk Island, in the Caribbean, John was escorted by Vice President Lyndon Johnson back to Florida, where he

The seven Mercury astronauts were honored with a ticker tape parade in New York after John's historic fight. John, Annie, and Vice President Lyndon Johnson are riding in the front car (inset). The front page of *The New York Times* headlined the story of John's space flight (background). At left is one of the buttons made to commemorate his flight.

AROUND THE WORLD IN 80 MINUTES
1st AMERICAN ASTRONAUT IN ORBIT
JOHN H. GLENN, JR.
WELCOME BACK TO EARTH

I felt I was there not just as a test-pilot-turned-astronaut who happened to have made America's first orbital space flight, but as a patriotic American with something to say about the space program and its embodiment of our nation's persistent quest to expand our knowledge and press forward our frontiers.

was reunited with his family. John hugged Dave and Lyn and couldn't hold back tears when he hugged and kissed Annie. After taking part in a parade at Cape Canaveral, the Glenn family spent several days enjoying being together again.

President Kennedy flew down to Cape Canaveral to welcome John back to Earth and to escort him to Washington, D.C., for a parade. John was also granted the rare privilege of addressing a joint session of Congress, where he talked about the importance of investing in space exploration. There were more speeches and parades, including a parade in New Concord and a ticker tape parade for John and the six other Mercury astronauts in New York City that was attended by an estimated four million people.

John was deluged with thousands of fan letters from people of every walk of life from around the globe. Even his hero, Charles Lindbergh, sent congratulations. Schools, roads, and newborn babies were named for John Glenn.

After the hoopla surrounding his space flight had died down, John went back to work at NASA. He soon tired of desk work and became impatient about when — and if — he would ever be scheduled for a second space flight. President Kennedy and his brother Attorney General Robert Kennedy encouraged him to enter politics and run for the Senate from Ohio. He was not ready to make this move, but the shocking assassination of President Kennedy on November 22, 1963, prompted John to reconsider his plans. He decided that he could best serve his country by being elected to public office.

In January 1964, John resigned from the astronaut corps and announced his intention to run for a seat in the U.S. Senate from Ohio. Soon after, a head injury caused by a fall forced him to leave the Senate race. In January 1965, John resigned from the Marine Corps and began a successful career as a businessman. He became a senior executive for Royal Crown Cola and also invested in several hotels. But he soon longed to return to public service.

John had developed a close friendship with Bobby Kennedy, who became a U.S. Senator from New York after his brother's assassination. John described

John addressed a joint session of Congress after his flight, a rare privilege usually reserved for foreign dignitaries. His speech was frequently interrupted by applause, whistles, and cheers. The U.S. Capitol stands in the background.

Bobby as "one of the most compassionate people I ever knew."When Bobby ran for the Democratic nomination for President in 1968, John campaigned for his friend, despite the disapproval of some of his business colleagues. And when Bobby was assassinated in Los Angeles after his upset victory in the California primary in June of that year, Bobby's wife, Ethel, asked John and Annie to take the Kennedy children back to their home in Virginia. The following morning, John and a neighbor had the sad duty of informing Bobby's children, as gently as they could, that their father was dead. It was, he later said, "one of the hardest things I ever did in my life."

In 1974, John finally succeeded in his third run for a Senate seat from Ohio. One of John's greatest campaign assets was his life partner and best friend, Annie, who ultimately overcame her severe stutter after extensive language training. She loved people, and her warmth and kindness never failed to leave a strong positive impression on the people she met.

John was as much a competitor in the political world as he was in everything else he did. He pursued his new role as a United States Senator with his usual determination and sense of responsibility. On the desk of his Senate office, John kept one of his father's old, worn eight-inch plumbing wrenches to serve as a reminder of who he was and where he came from.

Given his military background, it was not surprising that John had a particular interest in national security matters. One of his biggest concerns was the spread of nuclear weapons. John was a leader in the Senate in trying to limit the spread of these deadly weapons and played a key role in the passage of the 1978 Nuclear Non-Proliferation Act. He was also years ahead of most of his Senate colleagues in warning about the grave danger to U.S. national security from terrorists who might get their hands on such devices. While he was a strong supporter of the military, John, who had experienced the horrors of combat firsthand, was cautious about the use of force to solve problems.

Of the many other issues in which he immersed himself in the Senate, John had a special interest in trying to increase government efficiency.

In 1968, John's close friend Bobby Kennedy, the U.S. Senator from New York, ran for the Democratic Party's nomination for President. Here, John joins Bobby as he campaigns in California.

Bobby Kennedy believed that no matter how large a problem was, a way could always be found to make it better. It was this quality, more than any other, that attracted me to him, as a person and as a politician.

John, Annie, Lyn, and supporters celebrate John's 1974 election to the U.S. Senate, where he would represent the people of Ohio for an unprecedented four, six-year terms. One of his campaign buttons is shown below.

He sponsored legislation that created independent offices within the departments and agencies of the federal government that were responsible for trying to eliminate waste and abuse of funds. He also stressed the importance of research and education in moving America and its individual citizens forward.

On January 28, 1986, John and the rest of the country were shocked by one of the greatest disasters in the history of the U.S. space program. On that day, the space shuttle *Challenger* blew up shortly after liftoff, killing all seven astronauts on board. Senator Glenn traveled to Houston, Texas, to attend the memorial service for the deceased astronauts. Back in Washington, he assembled his Senate staff to share his impressions of the service. He discussed the importance and dangers

*People my age weren't really
expected to do much....
The idea of an ancient guy like me going
into space was exhilarating.*

of space flight and described the "missing man" aerial formation of jet fighters at the memorial service, which is performed as a tribute to those who die in service to the nation. Then John Glenn counseled his staff, "If you ever have an opportunity to do something bigger than yourself, seize the opportunity."

While preparing for a Senate debate on funding for the international space station in 1995, John came across NASA medical research that listed numerous physical changes, such as osteoporosis (loss of bone density) and changes in the muscle system, that have been observed in astronauts in the weightlessness of space. Astronauts recovered from these problems when they returned to Earth and experienced the force of gravity. Many of these side effects of space travel are similar to the problems people face as they grow older. After reading these reports, John wondered if a better understanding of the aging process could be gained by sending an older person into space.

John, NASA, and National Institute of Aging doctors were convinced that this research was critical, and he was keen on being the test case. John had never completely gotten over his disappointment at not being assigned to a second space flight. He doggedly lobbied the NASA leadership about being the guinea pig for a mission to explore the aging process. Once again, John's persistence paid off. He passed the most rigorous physical tests, and NASA determined that John's research proposal deserved to be explored. In January 1998, almost one year after he announced his intention to retire from the Senate, 76-year-old John Glenn was informed that he would be returning to space.

I thought I could make reasoned, principled decisions on the issues by learning the facts, keeping in close touch with my constituents, and finding a balance between their needs and those of the country as a whole.

Senator John Glenn discusses
national security issues with
members of his staff in his office
in the Hart Senate Office Building,
in Washington, D.C.

John demonstrates the shuttle simulator to (above, left to right) son Dave, grandson Daniel, daughter-in-law Karen, Annie, and grandson Zach.

John is fitted with weblike head gear (right) for a sleep-monitoring experiment in preparation for the shuttle mission, which was officially called STS-95.

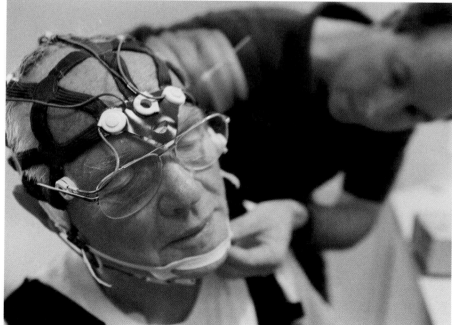

*The truth is, the old stereotypes
no longer fit, if ever they did.
Older people are increasingly active.
While the processes I was going to study
in space do tend to slow people down
as they age, increased longevity
and better health mean more older people
are doing more things than ever before.*

Some expressed concern about sending an individual of such an advanced age on a physically demanding space mission. But overcoming concerns about his age was not new for John. After he set a transcontinental speed record in 1957 as part of Project Bullet, *The New York Times* had expressed the opinion that "at 36, Major Glenn is reaching the practical age limit for piloting complicated pieces of machinery...." And John was 40 years old when he flew into space in 1962 as the oldest Mercury astronaut.

The space program had changed greatly since John's *Friendship 7* flight. It was no longer the domain of white male test pilots who came from small American towns. Besides test pilots, the 1990s astronaut corps was made up of engineers, scientists, and medical experts, many of whom were women and individuals of different nationalities with diverse ethnic backgrounds.

John's six crewmates on the space shuttle *Discovery* demonstrated this new diversity. Mission commander Curt Brown and pilot Steve Lindsey were lieutenant colonels in the Air Force and had conducted weapons systems testing; Steve Robinson had a Ph.D. in mechanical engineering; Scott Parazynski was a medical doctor; and Chiaki Mukai was a heart surgeon and the first Japanese woman in space. Except for first-time astronaut Pedro Duque of Spain, John's crewmates had more experience in space than he did.

As payload specialist number two, John was the lowest-ranking person on the seven-member crew. He enjoyed the flight training and was fascinated by the scientific experiments he was assigned to work on. John looked forward to experiencing weightlessness in the space shuttle, which was far more spacious than the cramped *Friendship 7* capsule.

John Glenn's return to space created enormous public excitement and attention in the media and rekindled the enthusiasm for and sense of purpose of space flight. The mission was particularly meaningful to people who remembered the flight of *Friendship 7*, inspiring them to continue leading full and active lives.

When John had first raised the possibility of returning to space, Annie had been cool to the idea. She had hoped that John's physical risk-taking had ended years ago in the Mercury program. But Annie knew how much the mission meant to her husband, so she observed his astronaut training in Houston, Texas, sat in on classes, and talked to the scientists regarding the aging experiments that were part of John's mission duties. She ultimately came to share John's enthusiasm about his return to space.

On October 29, 1998, more than 36 years after the flight of *Friendship 7*, John Glenn was headed back into space. When he told her yet one more time that he was going out to get a pack of gum, she said, "Don't be too long." As the space shuttle *Discovery* blasted off the launch pad, Mission Control announced, "Liftoff of *Discovery* with a crew of six astronaut heroes and one American legend." John's fellow Mercury astronaut Scott Carpenter was on hand to give him the same parting message he had offered on February 20, 1962: "Godspeed, John Glenn." At 77 years of age, John was the oldest human being ever to travel into space.

While it took time to adjust to weightlessness in the shuttle, John was exhilarated by the experience. Whenever there was a lull in his duties, he was at the shuttle's windows, staring at the spectacular view of Earth. John was the test case for a number of experiments on the aging process. During the flight, he gave numerous blood samples to evaluate his protein levels

A pillar of fire propels the shuttle *Discovery* into space on a clear October day in Florida (above). Commander Curt Brown reported when they reached orbit, "Let the record show that John has a smile on his face and it goes from one ear to the other and we haven't been able to remove it yet."

Joyous spectators (left) eagerly await John Glenn and the other returning *Discovery* astronauts during a ticker tape parade in New York.

Second-time astronaut John Glenn on a training flight.

*It was hard to imagine that virtually
the entire history of space travel had
occurred between my first ride and my second....
It didn't seem that long to me, but
that is the way lives pass when you look
back on them: in the blink of an eye.*

and his body's ability to protect itself from illness, and he was closely monitored for changes to his heart rhythms, breathing, bone density, muscles, sense of balance, and sleeping patterns. John also swallowed a pill thermometer the size of a large jelly bean that took temperature readings as it passed through his body. These and other tests were far more advanced than the experiments he had undertaken during his comparatively brief *Friendship 7* flight.

During his 1962 space flight, the space program was simply seeking to establish a baseline, or starting place, of information about human capabilities in the weightless environment of space. For example, during his Mercury flight, John successfully read a vision chart, demonstrating that eyeballs would not change shape in space and impair vision as had been feared. The medical tests on the *Discovery* were an effort to establish a different baseline of information, one that could lead one day to improving the quality of life for the elderly.

Nine days after launch, on November 7, 1998, *Discovery* landed safely on a runway at Cape Canaveral after traveling 3.6 million miles and making 134 Earth orbits. After his flight on *Discovery*, John stated with justifiable pride, "Going back to space, I had defied the expectations for my age."

I've looked at most of my life as public service.

Senator Glenn reviews a model for the renovation of The Ohio State University's Page Hall — site of the John Glenn Institute for Public Service and Public Policy — with University President Karen Holbrook and OSU students.

AFTERWORD

John Glenn's extraordinary space shuttle flight represented the crowning achievement of his public service career. Perhaps the most important finding from John's shuttle flight was the absence of significant differences between his physical reaction to launch, re-entry, and nine days of weightlessness and those of the younger astronauts on the flight. John's medical data from the flight will be evaluated for some time, and, with further research, could increase our ability to address the problems of aging.

John doesn't dwell on the past. He has continued to work to build a better world for future generations of Americans. The John Glenn Institute for Public Service and Public Policy at The Ohio State University in Columbus, houses John's papers and artifacts and makes them available to the public. Most important to John, the Institute is instructing young people about the significance and rewards of public service.

John has chaired commissions that sought to improve the quality of teaching in science and mathematics and to combine community service with classroom work as a way of teaching civic responsibility. Always dedicated to aviation, he played a prominent role in Dayton, Ohio's, 2003 celebration of the 100th anniversary of the Wright Brother's historic first powered flight. And as the spokesman for the construction of the new Visitor's Center for the U.S. Capitol, John was in the Capitol building on September 11, 2001, when terrorists attacked New York and the Pentagon, awakening the nation to a terrible new threat to its security. The shocking attacks made him regret not being in the Senate to help the country deal with the growing menace of terrorism.

If you ever have an opportunity to do something bigger than yourself, seize the opportunity.

John continues to speak out about various public policy issues. In 2004, he gave testimony to a Senate committee against a proposed amendment to the U.S. Constitution that would prohibit anyone from desecrating (treating disrespectfully) the American flag. While he is offended by anyone who would show any disrespect to the American flag, John believes that the First Amendment to the Constitution guarantees freedom of speech, particularly to those who express themselves in ways most Americans find offensive. He thinks that it is important to distinguish between the flag and the liberties the flag represents. "Those who have made the ultimate sacrifice and died following that banner did not give up their lives for a red, white and blue piece of cloth. They died because they went into harm's way representing this country and because of their allegiance to the values, the rights, and principles represented by that flag."

Speaking about the American flag, John says, "Our most revered symbol stands for freedom but is not freedom itself. We must not let those who revile our way of life trick us into diminishing our great gift, or even take a chance of diminishing our freedoms."

In a long and active life filled with significant service to his nation, John Glenn has inspired millions of people around the world—both young and old—not just with his words, but also by the eloquence of his example. His commitment to public service, his sense of duty, courage, integrity, and decency serve as a model to everyone who seeks to make the world a better place.

Memorabilia from John Glenn's lengthy and prominent public service career

CHRONOLOGY

1921
John Herschel Glenn, Jr., is born in Cambridge, Ohio, on July 18.

1939
Glenn enrolls in Muskingum College, New Concord, Ohio.

1941
He takes flying lessons at an airport outside New Philadelphia, Ohio, and earns his pilot's license.

1942
John drops out of college to enlist in the U.S. Navy and later transfers to the Marine Corps.

1943
He marries his childhood sweetheart, Anna (Annie) Margaret Castor, on April 6.

1944
John flies his first combat mission on July 10. He flies 59 fighter bomber missions in World War II.

1945
Son, David, is born on December 13.

1947
Daughter, Lyn, is born on March 19.

1953
John serves in the Korean War as a combat pilot.

1954
He is assigned to serve as a Marine test pilot at the Naval Air Test Center at Patuxent River, Maryland.

1956
He is assigned to the Fighter Design Branch of the Navy Bureau of Aeronautics (now Bureau of Naval Weapons) in Washington, D.C., from November 1956 until April 1959.

1957
John pilots Operation Bullet on July 16, setting a transcontinental speed record from Los Angeles to New York in 3 hours and 23 minutes.

1959
He is selected as one of the seven Project Mercury astronauts in April.

1962
After numerous delays, Glenn is launched into space in *Friendship 7* on February 20 and orbits the Earth three times.

In ceremonies in Washington, D.C., on April 9, Vice President Lyndon Johnson presents Glenn with the Hubbard Medal, the highest honor the National Geographic Society can bestow in the field of research and exploration.

1964
In January he resigns from NASA and enters the race to be the Democratic nominee for U.S. Senator from Ohio. An accident causes him to withdraw in March.

Glenn is promoted to the rank of Colonel in the U.S. Marine Corps in October.

1965
He retires from the Marine Corps on January 1 and becomes an executive for Royal Crown Cola Company.

1968
John campaigns for his friend Robert F. Kennedy, who is seeking the Democratic presidential nomination.

1974
John is elected as a U.S. Senator from Ohio in November and begins his first term on December 24.

1978
Glenn is the primary architect of the Nuclear Non-Proliferation Act.

1980
John is re-elected in November to a second term in the U.S. Senate.

1983
On April 21 in New Concord, Ohio, he announces his candidacy for the Democratic nomination for President of the United States.

1984
On March 16, he withdraws from the presidential race.

1986
He is re-elected in November to a third term in the U.S. Senate.

1988
In November, Glenn is one of 15 recipients of the National Geographic Society's Centennial Award. The recipients "epitomize the Society's century of commitment to and support of research and exploration."

1992
He is re-elected in November to an unprecedented fourth term as U.S. Senator from Ohio.

1998
The creation of The John Glenn Institute for Public Service and Public Policy at The Ohio State University is announced.

Shuttle Mission STS-95 *Discovery* is launched into space with Glenn on board on October 29 and returns to Earth on November 7.

1999
John retires from the U.S. Senate on January 3 after 24 years.

He is appointed Chairman of the National Commission on Mathematics and Science Teaching for the 21st Century to create a strategy to improve the quality of teaching in mathematics and science at all grades nationwide.

2000
He is appointed Chairman of the National Commission on Service-Learning—a teaching strategy that combines community service with classroom work to enhance learning and teach civic responsibility.

2003
He is appointed Secretary General of "Inventing Flight"—an organization in Dayton, Ohio, to celebrate the 100th anniversary of the first powered airplane flight by Dayton natives Wilbur and Orville Wright.

RESOURCE GUIDE

Books

Carpenter, M. Scott, L. Gordon Cooper, Jr., John H. Glenn, Jr., Virgil I. Grissom, Walter M. Schirra, Jr., Alan B. Shepard, Jr., and Donald K. Slayton. *We Seven.* New York: Simon & Schuster, 1962.

Carpenter, Scott and Kris Stoever. *For Spacious Skies: The Uncommon Journey of a Mercury Astronaut.* New York: New American Library, 2004.

Fenno, Jr., Richard F. *The Presidential Odyssey of John Glenn.* Washington, D.C.: CQ Press, 1990.

Glenn, John, ed. *"P.S. I listened to your heartbeat" Letters to John Glenn.* Houston: World Book Encyclopedia Science Service, Inc., 1964.

Glenn, John with Nick Taylor. *John Glenn: A Memoir.* New York: Bantam Books, 1999.

Godwin, Robert, ed. *FRIENDSHIP 7: The First Flight of John Glenn — The NASA Mission Reports.* Burlington, Ontario: Apogee Books, 1971.

Heatley, C.J., III (with Introduction by Senator John Glenn). *Forged in Steel: U.S. Marine Corps Aviation.* Charlottesville: Howell Press, Inc., 1987.

Kranz, Gene. *Failure Is NOT an Option: Mission Control From Mercury to Apollo 13 and Beyond.* New York: Simon & Schuster, 2000.

Montgomery, Scott and Timothy R. Gaffney. *Back in Orbit: John Glenn's Return to Space.* Atlanta: Longstreet Press, Inc., 1998.

Porter, Lorle (with Foreword by John Glenn). *Images of America: John Glenn's New Concord.* Chicago: Arcadia Publishing, 2001.

Shepard, Alan and Deke Slayton. *Moon Shot: The Inside Story of America's Race to the Moon.* Atlanta: Turner Publishing, Inc., 1994.

Van Riper, Frank. *Glenn — The Astronaut Who Would Be President.* New York: Empire Books, 1983.

Wolfe, Tom. *The Right Stuff.* New York: Farrar, Strauss, Giroux, 1979.

NATIONAL GEOGRAPHIC Articles

Fisher, Jr., Allan C. "Exploring Tomorrow with the Space Agency." (July 1960), 48–89.

Jackson, Jr., M.D., Carmault B. "The Flight of *Freedom 7.*" (September 1961), 416–431.

Newcott, William R. "John Glenn: Man with a Mission." (June 1999), 60–81.

Voas, Robert B. "John Glenn's Three Orbits in *Friendship 7*: A Minute-by-Minute Account of America's First Orbital Space Flight." (June 1962), 792–827.

Weaver, Kenneth F. "Countdown for Space." (May 1961), 702–734.

Weaver, Kenneth F. "Tracking America's Man in Orbit." (February 1962), 184–217.

Videos

ABC News. "Heaven and Earth First Step/with Peter Jennings." Stamford, CT: ABC Video, 1999.

KCET Hollywood and Newsweek Productions. "John Glenn American Hero." Alexandria, VA: PBS Home Video, 1998.

MPI Media Group. "John Glenn: An American Legend." MPI Home Video, 1998.

National Aeronautics and Space Administration. "*Friendship 7.*" Washington, D.C.: Westlake Entertainment Group, 1998.

Wheeler, Chris. "Godspeed, John Glenn." New York: Discovery Channel Video, 1998.

Recommended Web sites

The John and Annie Glenn Historic Site and Exploration Center, New Concord, Ohio
www.johnglennhome.org/index.shtml

The Ohio State University's The John Glenn Institute for Public Service and Public Policy, 350 Page Hall, 1810 College Road, Columbus, Ohio 43210
www.glenninstitute.org/glenn/index.asp

NASA's Kennedy Space Center overview of *Friendship 7* flight:
www.pao.ksc.nasa.gov/kscpao/history/mercury/ma-6/ma-6.htm

NASA's Kennedy Space Center overview of STS-95 Space Shuttle flight:
www.science.ksc.nasa.gov/shuttle/missions/sts-95/mission-sts-95.html

National Aeronautics and Space Administration (NASA):
www.nasa.gov/home

Smithsonian National Air and Space Museum
www.nasm.si.edu/

National Museum of the United States Air Force, Wright-Patterson Air Force Base, Ohio
www.wpafb.af.mil/museum/

About the Author

Don Mitchell has worked as a public servant for more than 20 years in the federal government, serving in the U.S. Senate as well as in the White House on the staff of the National Security Council. He worked on national security issues for Senator John Glenn for 15 years. Don and his wife, Grace, live in Arlington, Virginia, with their children, Logan Adlai and Ella Ruth.

INDEX

Photo credits

All images, except as noted below, are courtesy of the John Glenn Archives, The Ohio State University.

Front cover: Ralph Morse/Time Life Pictures/Getty Images (John Glenn); Getty Images (background). Back cover: Joe McNally/NG Image Collection (John Glenn); NASA (background).1, KSC/NASA; 5, Michael Rougier/Time Life Pictures/Getty Images; 6 (background), NASA; 6 (inset), Joe McNally/NG Image Collection; 11, Hulton Archive/Getty Images; 14 (bottom), WACO Historical Society; 26 (left), U.S. Navy; 27, NASA; 28, NASA; 29 (inset), NASA; 30, Sovfoto; 31, © Bettmann/Corbis; 32, Ralph Morse/Time Life Pictures/Getty Images; 33 (inset), KSC/NASA; (background) Courtesy Ron Grimes Collection; 34, © Bettmann/Corbis; 35 (background), KSC/NASA; 35 (inset), NASA; 36–37, NASA; 38–39, © NGS, based on map art by Irvin E. Alleman and Isaac Ortiz; 39 (bottom), Ralph Morse/Time Life Pictures/Getty Images; 40, © NGS, based on drawings by Robert W. Nicholson; 41, JSC/NASA; 42, Michael Rougier/ Time Life Pictures/Getty Images; 43 (background), *The New York Times*; 43 (center), © Corbis; 44 (inset), Ralph Morse/Time Life Pictures/Getty Images; (background) Digital Stock; 48 (top), Ralph Morse/Time Life Pictures/Getty Images; 48 (bottom), Courtesy Ron Grimes Collection; 50–51, David Hume Kennerly/Getty Images; 52 (top), David Hume Kennerly/Getty Images; 52 (bottom), Joe McNally/ NG Image Collection; 55 (top, and case cover), AFP/Getty Images; 55 (bottom), Joe McNally/ NG Image Collection; 56, Joe McNally, NG Image Collection; 58, The John Glenn Institute; 61, Photo by Gregory Heisler/ Time Inc./Time Life Pictures/Getty Images (*Time* cover); Courtesy Collection of the Author (pennant); Courtesy Ron Grimes Collection (memorabilia).

One of the world's largest non-profit scientific and educational organizations, the National Geographic Society was founded in 1888 "for the increase and diffusion of geographic knowledge." Fulfilling this mission, the Society educates and inspires millions every day through its magazines, books, television programs, videos, maps and atlases, research grants, the National Geographic Bee, teacher workshops, and innovative classroom materials. The Society is supported through membership dues, charitable gifts, and income from the sale of its educational products. This support is vital to National Geographic's mission to increase global understanding and promote conservation of our planet through exploration, research, and education.

For more information, please call 1-800-NGS LINE (647-5463) or write to the following address:

NATIONAL GEOGRAPHIC SOCIETY
1145 17th Street N.W.
Washington, D.C. 20036-4688
U.S.A.

Visit the Society's Web site:
www.nationalgeographic.com